MW01482619

ST. FRANCIS
OF ASSISI
THE HUMBLE SERVANT OF GOD

DR. LEO LEXICON

LEXICON LABS

LEXICON LABS TITLE LIST

STEM TITLES

Python for Teens: A Step-by-Step Guide
QUANTUM COMPUTING for Smart Pre-Teens and Teens Ages 10-19
PHYSICS NERD: 1000+ Amazing And Mind-Blowing Facts About Physics
BIOLOGY NERD: 1000+ Amazing And Mind-Blowing Facts About Biology
CHEMISTRY NERD: 1000+ Amazing And Mind-Blowing Facts About Chemistry
ASTRONOMY NERD: 1000+ Amazing And Mind-Blowing Facts About Astronomy
AI for Smart Kids Ages 6-9: Discover How Artificial Intelligence is Changing the World
Code Breakers: A Practical Guide to Mastering Programming Languages and Algorithms
Quantum Nerd Quizmaster Edition: Quantum Quizzes that Educate, Entertain and Challenge
The AI Nerd: Quizmaster Edition Mind-Blowing AI Quizzes that Educate, Entertain and Challenge
AI for Smart Pre-Teens and Teens Ages 10-19: Using Artificial Intelligence to Learn, Think, and Create
(Spanish Translation)LA IA ESTÁ AQUÍ: Usa la Inteligencia Artificial para Aprender, Pensar y Crear

ENTREPRENEURSHIP
10 Life Hacks Every Teen Should Know
Innovation Handbook for Teen Entrepreneurs
Teen Innovators: 30 Teen Trailblazers and their Breakthrough Ideas

GREAT SCIENTISTS SERIES
Nikola Tesla: An Electrifying Genius
John von Neumann: The Giga Brain
Einstein: The Man, The Myth, The Legend
Newton: Genius of the Scientific Revolution
Darwin: Unlocking the Secrets of Evolution
Richard Feynman: The Adventures of a Curious Physicist

GREAT INNOVATORS SERIES
Elon: A Modern Renaissance Man
Steve Jobs: The Visionary Innovator of Silicon Valley

GREAT LEADERS SERIES
Cleopatra: Queen of the Nile
Gandhi: Freedom Fighter and Global Icon
Churchill: The Spirit of an Indomitable Leader
Ben Franklin: Innovator, Statesman, Visionary
Lincoln: Emancipator and Defender of the Union
George Washington: The First American President
Mark Antony: The Rise and Tragic Fall of a Roman Legend
Jefferson: Statesman, Visionary and the Third US President
Julius Caesar: The Rise and Fall of Rome's Greatest Leader

GREAT EXPLORERS SERIES
Lewis and Clark: Blazing a Trail to the West
Magellan: First Circumnavigator of the Earth
Shackleton: Pioneering Explorer of the Antarctic
Robert Falcon Scott: A Pioneer of Antarctic Exploration
Marco Polo: Intrepid Explorer who Bridged East and West
Captain Cook: The Legendary Seafarer, Navigator, and Explorer

ST. FRANCIS OF ASSISI

The Humble Servant of God

Explore the life and legacy of St. Francis of Assisi, a beloved figure known for his profound humility, love for all creatures, and dedication to a life of poverty and service. This book provides an in-depth look at the life of St. Francis, from his early years and conversion to his establishment of the Franciscan Order and enduring impact on Christianity and the world.

St. Francis of Assisi was a man of extraordinary faith, compassion, and simplicity, whose actions and teachings continue to inspire millions. This book delves into his spiritual journey, his relationship with nature, and his unwavering commitment to living out the Gospel. From his youthful exuberance to his later years of leading a religious movement, St. Francis' story is a powerful testament to the transformative power of faith and love.

What You Will Learn

Francis' Early Life and Conversion:

- Discover how Francis' upbringing and early experiences led to a profound spiritual transformation.

Embracing Poverty and Service:

- Follow Francis' journey of renouncing wealth and embracing a life of poverty and service to others.

Establishment of the Franciscan Order:
- Understand the founding of the Franciscan Order and its impact on the Church and society.

Francis' Teachings and Writings:
- Explore the teachings and writings of St. Francis, including his famous "Canticle of the Sun."

Legacy and Influence:
- Examine the enduring legacy of St. Francis and his influence on Christianity, environmentalism, and social justice.

Written in an engaging and accessible style, this book is ideal for readers seeking a deeper understanding of one of history's most beloved saints. Each chapter provides a comprehensive look at Francis' life and achievements, making complex historical and spiritual events accessible and fascinating.

Why St. Francis of Assisi Matters Today

In a world increasingly focused on material wealth and power, St. Francis' life offers profound lessons in humility, compassion, and environmental stewardship. This book encourages readers to reflect on their values and actions, and to consider the transformative power of faith and simplicity.

Extras for the Curious Mind

The book also includes:

- **Glossary of Terms and Concepts:** Clarifies important terms and events related to Francis' life and the Franciscan movement.
- **Timeline of Francis' Life and Key Events:** Provides a chronological overview of significant milestones.
- **Further Reading and Resources:** Suggests additional materials for those interested in exploring the broader context of Francis' era.

Join the Exploration

"St. Francis of Assisi: The Humble Servant of God" is an immersive journey into the life of a man who embodied the spirit of Christian love and humility. Join us in examining the achievements and challenges of St. Francis, and discover how his legacy continues to inspire and inform believers and seekers today.

Dr. Leo Lexicon is an educator and author. He is the founder of Lexicon Labs, a publishing imprint that is focused on creating entertaining and educational books for active minds.

Saint Francis of Assisi
by Antoniazzo Romano (Antonio di Benedetto Aquilio), ca. 1480–81
(Source: Metropolitan Museum of Art, New York)

CONTENTS

Chapter 1

The Call to Conversion

A Transformational Experience

In the later years of his life, the man we now know as St. Francis of Assisi experienced a profoundly challenging and transformative event that would mark the culmination of his spiritual journey. It was in September 1224, while seeking solitude and deeper communion with God on Mount La Verna, that Francis received the stigmata, the wounds of Christ, on his hands, feet, and side. This mystical experience was both a blessing and a burden, signifying his complete identification with the suffering of Christ.

Francis had retreated to Mount La Verna for a period of fasting and prayer in preparation for the Feast of St. Michael. During this time, he fervently prayed to share in the suffering of Christ, yearning to experience the depth of his Savior's sacrifice. One morning, as he was deep in contemplation, Francis saw a vision of a seraph, an

1

angelic being, crucified like Jesus. As the vision faded, he felt an intense pain and saw that his body bore the marks of crucifixion.

This extraordinary event had a profound impact on Francis. Physically, the wounds caused him great pain and suffering, but spiritually, they brought him immense joy and a sense of divine closeness. The stigmata became a visible testament to his devotion and sanctity, reinforcing his message of humility, poverty, and love for all creation. Despite the physical agony, Francis continued to preach and serve others, embodying the spirit of Christ's love and sacrifice until his death in 1226.

But the story of St. Francis begins long before this divine encounter, in the bustling city of Assisi where he was born and raised.

Family Background and Upbringing

In the bustling Italian city of Assisi, a child was born to a wealthy cloth merchant and his French noblewoman wife in the year 1181 or 1182. This child, named Giovanni di Pietro di Bernardone, would one day become known to the world as St. Francis of Assisi, a man whose life and teachings would inspire millions across the centuries. Francis' father, Pietro di Bernardone, was a successful businessman who traveled frequently to France for trade. It was during one of these trips that Francis was born, and upon Pietro's return, he renamed his son Francesco, or "the Frenchman," in honor of his love for France. Growing up, Francis enjoyed a privileged life, as his family's wealth afforded him the finest clothes, education, and social connections.

Fig. The Mountain Town of Assisi

As a youth, Francis was known for his charm, generosity, and love of adventure. He dreamed of becoming a knight and winning glory on the battlefield, a path that many young men of his station aspired to. His father, who had grand ambitions for his son, encouraged these dreams, hoping that Francis would one day bring honor to the family name.

However, beneath the surface of this seemingly idyllic childhood, there were hints of the deep spiritual yearning that would later consume Francis. He was known to slip away from the revelry of his friends to pray in solitude, and he had a particular compassion for the poor and sick, often giving them alms or offering them comfort.

As Francis grew into a young man, his life took a dramatic turn when Assisi became embroiled in a conflict with the neighboring city of Perugia. Eager to prove himself, Francis joined the cavalry and rode out to battle, only to be captured and imprisoned for a year. This experience, coupled with a subsequent illness, sparked a profound spiritual crisis in Francis, one that would set him on the path to becoming one of the most revered saints in Christian history.

Influences and Education

Francis' education was typical for a young man of his social class in medieval Italy. He likely received tutoring in Latin, the language of the Church and scholarship, as well as instruction in reading, writing, and arithmetic. As the son of a merchant, he would have also learned the skills necessary for trade and business.

However, Francis' true education came from the vibrant world around him. Assisi was a hub of cultural and intellectual activity, and Francis was exposed to a wide range of influences, from the troubadours and poets who entertained in the squares to the religious orders who tended to the poor and sick.

One of the most significant influences on Francis during this time was the growing movement of lay piety. In response to the perceived corruption and worldliness of the Church, many lay people sought to live out the Gospel message in their daily lives, embracing poverty, simplicity, and service to others. This movement, which would later give rise to the Franciscan Order, had a profound impact on Francis' spiritual development.

Another key influence was the cult of chivalry, which celebrated the ideals of courage, honor, and courtly love. As a young man, Francis was enamored with these ideals, and they shaped his early aspirations and behavior. He dreamed of being a great knight, winning glory and the love of a noble lady.

However, as Francis matured, he began to question the values of his society. He saw the stark inequality between the rich and the poor, the suffering of the sick and outcast, and the futility of worldly ambition. These observations, coupled with his own spiritual experiences, would eventually lead him to reject the path of wealth and status and embrace a life of radical poverty and service.

Youthful Exuberance and Aspirations

As a young man, Francis was known for his love of pleasure and adventure. He was a leader among his peers, known for his wit, generosity, and flamboyant style. He loved fine clothes, good food and wine, and the company of friends.

One of Francis' great aspirations was to become a knight and win glory on the battlefield. This was a common dream for young men of his social class, who were raised on tales of chivalry and heroism. Francis' father, who had grand ambitions for his son, encouraged these dreams, hoping that military success would bring honor and status to the family.

In pursuit of this dream, Francis eagerly joined the cavalry when Assisi went to war with Perugia. He imagined himself returning home a hero, celebrated by his fellow citizens and admired by all. However, the reality of war was far different from the romanticized tales he had grown up with.

Francis was quickly captured by the enemy and spent a year in a dark, dank prison cell. This experience, along with a subsequent illness, forced Francis to confront the fragility of life and the emptiness of his worldly ambitions. He began to question the values he had once held so dear, and to seek a deeper meaning and purpose.

Upon his release, Francis returned to Assisi a changed man. He no longer cared for the revelry and vanity of his former life. Instead, he withdrew into solitude, spending long hours in prayer and contemplation. He began to feel a growing compassion for the poor and marginalized, seeing in them the face of Christ.

This shift in Francis' priorities did not sit well with his father, who had hoped his son would follow in his footsteps as a successful merchant. Pietro di Bernardone saw Francis' behavior as a rejection of all he had provided for him, and a threat to the family's social standing. The tension between father and son would eventually come to a dramatic head, setting the stage for Francis' ultimate conversion.

Social Life and Ambitions

Before his conversion, Francis was a popular figure in Assisi's social scene. His family's wealth and his own charisma made him a sought-after companion at feasts, parties, and other gatherings. He was known for his love of French troubadour songs and his skill in singing and dancing.

Francis' social life was closely tied to his ambitions. As a young man, he dreamed of being a great knight, winning glory and fame on the battlefield. He saw military success as a way to gain status and respect in society, and to prove himself worthy of a noble lady's love.

These ambitions were not unusual for a young man of Francis' background. In medieval Italy, the ideals of chivalry and courtly love were highly prized, and many young men aspired to live out these ideals. Francis, with his love of adventure and romance, was particularly drawn to this world.

However, Francis' experiences in war and prison began to change his perspective. He saw firsthand the suffering caused by violence and conflict, and he began to question the value of worldly glory. His subsequent illness also forced him to confront his own mortality and the fleeting nature of earthly pleasures.

As Francis grappled with these realizations, his social life and ambitions began to shift. He withdrew from the revelry and excess of his former companions, preferring solitude and contemplation. He began to associate with the poor and marginalized, finding in them a more authentic expression of Christian love.

This change in Francis' behavior did not go unnoticed. His friends and family were puzzled and even alarmed by his new priorities. His father, in particular, saw Francis' actions as a threat to the family's social standing and future prospects. The tension between Francis' old life and his new calling would eventually lead to a dramatic break with his past, and the beginning of his life as a humble servant of God.

Call to Conversion

The pivotal moment in Francis' conversion came in the year 1205, as he was praying before a crucifix in the dilapidated church of San Damiano. As Francis gazed upon the image of Christ, he heard a voice speak to him, saying, "Francis, go and repair my house, which, as you see, is falling into ruin."

At first, Francis took this command literally. He began to physically rebuild the church of San Damiano, using stones and materials begged from the people of Assisi. However, as he worked, he began to realize that the "house" Christ spoke of was not just the physical church, but the Church as a whole, which Francis saw as corrupt and in need of spiritual renewal.

This realization marked a profound shift in Francis' life. He began to see his true calling not as a knight or merchant, but as a servant of God and the poor. He started to embrace a life of radical poverty, giving away his possessions and living among the marginalized.

One of the key moments in this transformation was Francis' encounter with a leper. In medieval society, lepers were highly stigmatized and often forced to live in isolation. Francis, who had always had a strong aversion to lepers, one day came across one on the road outside Assisi.

In a moment of grace, Francis overcame his revulsion and embraced the leper, kissing his wounds. This act of compassion marked a profound change in Francis' heart. He began to see Christ in the face of the poor and suffering, and to understand that true joy and fulfillment lay in serving others.

As Francis continued on his path of conversion, he faced significant challenges and opposition. His father, angry at his son's rejection of wealth and status, publicly disowned him. Many in Assisi saw Francis' behavior as bizarre and even scandalous.

However, Francis remained steadfast in his commitment to living out the Gospel. He began to preach in the streets, calling people to repentance and a life of simplicity and love. His message and example began to attract followers, laying the groundwork for what would become the Franciscan Order.

Let us end this Chapter by consider ten lesser-known facts about St. Francis

1. Before his conversion, Francis was an aspiring troubadour and loved to sing French songs.
2. He had a particular fondness for animals, and is said to have preached to the birds.
3. Francis created the first live nativity scene in 1223 in the town of Greccio.

4. He was never ordained as a priest, remaining a deacon throughout his life.

5. Francis had a special devotion to the Eucharist and would often spend entire nights in prayer before the Blessed Sacrament.

6. He composed the famous "Canticle of the Sun" in the local Umbrian dialect, rather than in Latin.

7. Francis had a great love for France, and even attempted a pilgrimage there, though he never reached his destination.

8. He was known to sometimes preach in the nude, as a sign of his complete renunciation of worldly goods.

9. Francis had a scar on his right eyelid from a battle injury sustained in his youth.

10. He died on October 3, 1226, at the age of 44, in the church of the Portiuncula, the little chapel he had rebuilt after hearing Christ's call.

Chapter 2

Embracing Poverty and Service

Living Among the Poor

After his profound spiritual awakening, Francis made the radical decision to live among the poor and marginalized of Assisi. He abandoned his comfortable life and privileged status, choosing instead to identify with those on the fringes of society.

This was a shocking move in a time when social hierarchies were rigidly defined and those born into wealth were expected to maintain their status. Francis' family and friends were appalled by his actions, seeing them as a rejection of all they held dear. But for Francis himself, living among the poor was a natural expression of his newfound understanding of the Gospel. He saw in the face of each beggar, each leper, each outcast, the face of Christ himself. By serving them, he believed he was serving God directly.

Francis took to begging for his own food, a practice that was deeply humbling for someone of his background. He often gave away what little he had to those in greater need, trusting in God's providence for his own sustenance.

This lifestyle was not without its challenges. Francis faced ridicule, rejection, and even physical danger. Many saw his behavior as madness, a sign of a deranged mind. Others were threatened by his example, which called into question their own attachment to wealth and status.

Yet Francis persevered, finding joy and freedom in his new way of life. He discovered a deep sense of solidarity with the poor, a shared humanity that transcended social divisions. In their struggles, he saw his own; in their joys, he found cause for celebration.

As word of Francis' way of life spread, others began to be drawn to his example. Men from various walks of life, moved by his radical witness, started to join him in his life of poverty and service. This small band of brothers would form the nucleus of what would eventually become the Franciscan Order.

Through his living example, Francis challenged the assumptions of his time about the value and dignity of human life. He demonstrated that true joy and fulfillment come not from wealth or status, but from loving and serving others, especially those most in need. His witness continues to inspire people of all faiths to this day to see the face of God in the poor and marginalized.

Acts of Charity and Service

Francis' commitment to poverty was not a passive one. He actively sought out ways to serve and care for those in need, seeing this as an essential part of his spiritual calling.

One of the most striking examples of this was his care for lepers. In medieval society, leprosy was a highly stigmatized disease, and those afflicted were often forced to live in isolation, cut off from family and community. They were seen as unclean, physically and spiritually, and were often treated with fear and revulsion.

Francis, however, saw in lepers the suffering Christ. He went out of his way to visit them, to bring them food and comfort, to wash their wounds and kiss their sores. This was a shocking act in a time when most people would go out of their way to avoid any contact with lepers.

For Francis, this was not an act of extraordinary heroism, but a simple expression of Christian love. He saw no distinction between serving lepers and serving Christ; they were one and the same.

Francis' care for lepers was part of a broader pattern of service to the sick and suffering. He and his early followers would often visit hospitals and hospices, offering comfort and care to the patients. They would beg for food and other necessities to distribute to the needy.

Francis also had a special concern for the spiritual welfare of those he served. He would preach to them, sharing the message of God's love and the promise of eternal life. For many of the poor and sick, this spiritual nourishment was as vital as the physical care they received.

Through these acts of charity and service, Francis and his followers lived out the Gospel call to love one's neighbor. They demonstrated that this love is not abstract or sentimental, but concrete and practical, expressed in acts of compassion and care for those most in need.

This example of active, engaged love has inspired countless others over the centuries to follow in Francis' footsteps. Today, Franciscans and other followers of Francis continue his work of serving the poor, the sick, and the marginalized, seeing in them the face of Christ.

Building a Community

As Francis continued his life of poverty and service, he began to attract followers who were inspired by his example and wanted to share in his way of life. These early companions came from diverse backgrounds - some were wealthy and educated, others were poor and illiterate. What united them was a desire to live out the Gospel in a radical way, following in the footsteps of Christ.

One of the first to join Francis was Bernard of Quintavalle, a wealthy nobleman who was struck by Francis' example. He sold all his possessions, gave the money to the poor, and joined Francis in his life of poverty. Others soon followed, including Peter Catani and Giles of Assisi.

As the number of followers grew, Francis saw the need for some form of organization and rule of life. He was hesitant at first, fearing that too much structure would compromise the radical simplicity and freedom of their way of life.

However, he also recognized the need for order and stability if this way of life was to endure. With input from his early companions, Francis drew up a simple rule of life, based on the Gospel. This rule emphasized poverty, chastity, and obedience, as well as a commitment to prayer, preaching, and service to the poor.

This early community was marked by a strong sense of fraternity and mutual care. They saw each other as true brothers, united in their love for Christ and their desire to follow him. They shared all things in common, owning no property individually but depending on the generosity of others and their own labor for their needs.

The brothers would often go out in pairs to preach and serve, spreading the message of the Gospel and the example of their way of life. They relied on the hospitality of those they met for their food and shelter, trusting in God's providence.

As the community grew, it began to spread beyond Assisi. Francis sent brothers out to other parts of Italy and even beyond, to France,

Spain, Germany, and the Holy Land. Wherever they went, they lived and preached in the same simple, humble way, attracting others to join them.

This growing movement was not without its challenges. Some within the Church hierarchy were suspicious of this new form of religious life, which seemed to challenge traditional monastic models. There were also internal struggles as the community tried to balance its commitment to poverty and simplicity with the practical needs of a growing organization.

Through it all, Francis remained the guiding spirit, reminding his brothers of their original calling and inspiration. Even as he stepped back from formal leadership in his later years, his example and teachings continued to shape the community he had founded.

Today, the Franciscan family includes not only the First Order of friars, but also the Second Order of the Poor Clares (the female branch founded by St. Clare under Francis' guidance), and the Third Order of lay Franciscans. This global community continues to live out Francis' vision in a variety of ways, adapted to the needs and challenges of the modern world.

Preaching and Teaching

Alongside his commitment to poverty and service, Francis was also dedicated to preaching and sharing the message of the Gospel. He saw this as an essential part of his calling, a way to invite others into the joy and freedom he had found in following Christ.

Francis' approach to preaching was unconventional for his time. In an era when most preaching was done by educated clerics in Latin, Francis preached in the vernacular, using simple stories and images that ordinary people could understand. He often used dramatic gestures and even props to get his message across.

One famous example of this was when he preached to a flock of birds. According to tradition, Francis came across a large group of birds while walking and began to preach to them about God's love and care for all creatures. To the amazement of his companions, the birds seemed to listen attentively and did not fly away until Francis had finished.

Whether or not this specific event occurred as described, it captures something essential about Francis' approach. He had a deep sense of the sacredness of all creation and saw every creature as a bearer of God's love and beauty. His preaching was an invitation to see the world with new eyes, to recognize the presence of God in all things.

Francis' message was deeply rooted in the Gospel. He constantly called people back to the example and teachings of Jesus, especially his emphasis on love, humility, and service. He challenged his listeners to let go of their attachments to wealth, status, and power, and to find their true joy in following Christ.

At the same time, Francis' preaching was never judgmental or condemning. He had a deep compassion for human weakness and sin, recognizing it in himself as much as in others. His message was always one of invitation and encouragement, calling people to conversion and new life.

As the Franciscan community grew, Francis encouraged his brothers to continue this preaching ministry. They would often go out in pairs, traveling from town to town, preaching in marketplaces, churches, and wherever people gathered. Their simple, joyful witness was a powerful attraction, drawing many to follow their example.

Francis also recognized the importance of teaching within the community. He wanted his brothers to be grounded in prayer and the study of Scripture, so that their preaching would flow from a deep spiritual life. While he was sometimes wary of the pursuit of academic learning for its own sake, he valued education in service of the Gospel.

In his famous "Canticle of the Sun," Francis used the language of poetry and praise to teach about God's love and the wonder of creation. This same spirit of joyful, creative teaching characterized the early Franciscan movement.

Today, Franciscans continue this ministry of preaching and teaching in a variety of contexts, from universities and parishes to soup kitchens and homeless shelters. In a world that often seems divided and despairing, the Franciscan message of joy, simplicity, and love remains as vital as ever.

Chapter 3

The Franciscan Order

Founding the Order

As Francis' community of followers grew, it became clear that some form of official recognition and structure would be necessary for the movement to endure. Francis, always humble and submissive to the Church, decided to seek papal approval for his way of life.

In 1209 or 1210, Francis and a small group of his brothers traveled to Rome to meet with Pope Innocent III. This was a daring move, as Francis' radical vision of poverty and itinerant preaching could be seen as a challenge to the established order of the Church.

According to tradition, the Pope had a dream the night before meeting Francis. In this dream, he saw the Lateran Basilica, the cathedral church of Rome, on the verge of collapse. But then a small, humble man appeared and supported the church with his own back, preventing its fall. When Francis arrived the next day, the Pope recognized him as the man from his dream.

Whether or not this story is historically accurate, it captures the significance of the moment. The Pope, seeing the sincerity and faith of Francis and his companions, gave verbal approval to their way of life and granted them permission to preach.

This event marked the official founding of the Franciscan Order. The brothers now had the Church's blessing to live according to their rule of poverty, chastity, and obedience, and to preach the Gospel throughout the world.

This approval was a crucial step in the development of the Franciscan movement. It provided legitimacy and protection, allowing the Order to grow and spread without fear of being condemned as heretical or subversive.

At the same time, it marked a new phase in Francis' own journey. He was now not just the leader of a small band of companions, but the founder of an officially recognized religious order. This brought new responsibilities and challenges, as he had to guide the growing community and ensure it remained true to its original charism.

In the years that followed, Francis would continue to lead by example, living out his commitment to poverty, humility, and love. He would also work to refine and codify the rule of life for his brothers, seeking to balance the radical ideals of the Gospel with the practical needs of a growing community.

The founding of the Franciscan Order was a pivotal moment not just for Francis and his followers, but for the Church and the world. It marked the birth of a new form of religious life, one that would have a profound impact on spirituality, culture, and society for centuries to come.

Today, the Franciscan family includes multiple branches and tens of thousands of members worldwide. While the Order has evolved and diversified over the centuries, it continues to draw inspiration from the example and teachings of its humble founder, seeking to live out the Gospel in a spirit of simplicity, service, and joy.

Approval of the Rule by Pope Innocent III

The papal approval of Francis' way of life in 1209/1210 was a significant step, but it was not the end of the story. As the Franciscan community grew and developed, it became clear that a more detailed and formalized rule would be necessary to govern the life of the Order.

Francis, always submissive to the Church hierarchy, worked diligently to draft a rule that would encapsulate the key principles of Franciscan life while also being acceptable to the Pope and the Church authorities.

The first attempt at a written rule, known as the "Primitive Rule" or "Rule of 1221," was a simple, Gospel-based document. It emphasized poverty, humility, and service, and included practical guidelines for the daily life of the brothers.

However, this early rule was seen by some Church officials as too vague and potentially open to misinterpretation. There were concerns that the emphasis on radical poverty could lead to instability or even heresy if not properly regulated.

Francis, in his characteristic spirit of obedience, accepted these concerns and set about revising the rule. He sought the advice and input of learned brothers within the Order, as well as Church authorities.

The result was the "Later Rule" or "Rule of 1223." This version was more juridical in tone, with clearer regulations around issues such as poverty, the admission of new members, and the governance of the Order. It also included a stronger emphasis on obedience to the Church hierarchy.

This revised rule was submitted to Pope Honorius III (who had succeeded Innocent III) for approval. After some minor modifications, the Pope solemnly approved the rule on November 29, 1223, with the papal bull "Solet annuere."

This approval was a milestone for the Franciscan Order. It provided a clear and authoritative framework for Franciscan life, one that would guide the Order for centuries to come.

At the same time, the process of drafting and approving the rule highlighted some of the tensions that would continue to shape the Franciscan story. There was an ongoing balancing act between the radical ideals of Francis and the practical needs and expectations of the institutional Church.

Francis himself sometimes struggled with these tensions. He was always obedient to Church authority, but he also had a deep commitment to the absolute poverty and simplicity of the Gospel. Reconciling these two commitments was not always easy.

Nevertheless, the approval of the 1223 rule was a crucial step in solidifying the Franciscan way of life. It ensured that the Order had a stable foundation and could continue to grow and flourish within the structures of the Church.

Today, the Rule of 1223 remains the fundamental governing document for the Franciscan First Order (the Order of Friars Minor). While it has been supplemented by additional constitutions and interpretations over the centuries, it still provides the essential framework for Franciscan religious life.

The approval of this rule is a testament to Francis' humility, his obedience to the Church, and his dedication to ensuring that his vision of Gospel living could endure and bear fruit long after his own lifetime. It is one of the key legacies of his extraordinary life and leadership.

Growth and Expansion

With papal approval and a formalized rule, the Franciscan Order was poised for significant growth and expansion. In the years following the official founding of the Order, the number of friars increased dramatically, and Franciscan communities began to spread throughout Italy and beyond.

One of the key factors in this rapid growth was the appeal of the Franciscan way of life. In a time when the Church was often seen as wealthy and power-hungry, the friars' commitment to poverty, simplicity, and service was a powerful witness. Many men, from all walks of life, were drawn to this radical vision of Gospel living.

As the Order grew, Francis sent friars out to establish new communities. These early Franciscan missions often involved traveling to new cities or regions, preaching in the streets and marketplaces, and attracting new followers.

The friars would typically establish themselves in the poorest areas of a town, living among the people and serving their needs. They would rely on alms for their basic necessities, trusting in God's providence and the generosity of the faithful.

Over time, these initial settlements would develop into more established communities, with simple dwellings and places of worship. The friars would continue their ministry of preaching, service to the poor and sick, and pastoral care for the local population.

The expansion of the Order was not limited to Italy. Even during Francis' lifetime, Franciscan missions were established in other parts of Europe, including France, Spain, Germany, and England. Friars also traveled to the Holy Land, seeking to live and preach among the people there.

This international growth brought new challenges and opportunities. The friars had to adapt to different cultural and linguistic contexts, and navigate complex political and religious landscapes. At the same time, the spread of the Franciscan charism across borders was a powerful witness to the universality of the Gospel message.

As the Order grew, it also began to diversify. While all Franciscans shared a common commitment to poverty, humility, and service, different emphases and interpretations of the rule began to emerge. Some friars prioritized contemplative prayer and solitude, while others focused on active preaching and service.

This diversity would eventually lead to the emergence of distinct branches within the Franciscan family. The Order of Friars Minor (O.F.M.), which traces its lineage directly to Francis, would be joined by the Order of Friars Minor Conventual (O.F.M. Conv.) and the Order of Friars Minor Capuchin (O.F.M. Cap.), each with its own particular charism and way of life.

Despite these divisions, the core Franciscan ideals continued to inspire and attract new followers. The Order became one of the largest and most influential in the Church, with a significant presence in virtually every part of the Catholic world.

Today, the Franciscan family remains a vital part of the global Church. Franciscan friars, sisters, and lay associates continue to live out Francis' vision in a wide variety of contexts, from urban homeless shelters to remote mission outposts. The growth and expansion set in motion during those early years continues to bear fruit, touching countless lives with the joy and simplicity of the Gospel.

Internal and External Challenges

As the Franciscan Order grew and developed, it faced a number of internal challenges and external opposition. These tensions were in many ways inherent to the Franciscan charism itself, which sought to balance radical ideals with practical realities.

One of the primary internal challenges was the interpretation and application of the rule, particularly around the issue of poverty. Francis' vision of total renunciation of property and reliance on alms was a central part of the Franciscan way of life. However, as the Order grew, this radical poverty became more difficult to sustain.

Some friars argued for a stricter interpretation of poverty, insisting that the Order should not have any communal property at all. Others advocated for a more moderate approach, allowing for the use of property and resources as long as individual friars did not claim ownership.

These debates sometimes led to divisions and conflicts within the Order. In the later years of Francis' life, and especially after his death, different factions emerged, each claiming to be the true heirs of Francis' vision.

Another internal challenge was the balance between contemplation and action. Some friars felt called to a more solitary, prayer-focused life, while others emphasized active preaching and service. Finding a way to honor both of these aspects of the Franciscan charism was an ongoing struggle.

The Order also faced external opposition and criticism. Some Church leaders were wary of the Franciscans' radical approach to poverty and their emphasis on lay preaching. There were concerns that the friars might be spreading heretical ideas or undermining the authority of the clergy.

There were also tensions with some secular authorities, who saw the friars as a disruptive force. The Franciscans' critique of wealth and power, and their advocacy for the poor and marginalized, could be seen as a threat to the established social order.

Despite these challenges, the Franciscan Order continued to grow and thrive. Many Church leaders recognized the genuine holiness and positive impact of the Franciscan way of life. Popes and bishops often called upon the friars for various ministries and missions, recognizing their unique gifts and charism.

The friars also had a significant impact on the wider culture. Franciscan spirituality, with its emphasis on simplicity, joy, and love of creation, resonated deeply with many people. Franciscan art, literature, and science made significant contributions to the intellectual and cultural life of medieval Europe.

Internally, the Order continued to wrestle with the challenges of living out Francis' vision in a changing world. Various reforms and renewal movements emerged over the centuries, seeking to recapture the original Franciscan spirit.

Today, these challenges and tensions continue in new forms. Franciscans around the world seek to adapt their charism to the needs of the contemporary Church and world, while remaining faithful to the core ideals of their founder.

The ongoing story of the Franciscan Order is one of both struggle and resilience, of human weakness and divine grace. Through all the challenges and opposition, the simple, joyful witness of Francis and his followers continues to inspire and transform lives, calling all people to a deeper embrace of the Gospel.

Vision Versus Reality

At the heart of the Franciscan story is the tension between Francis' radical vision and the practical realities of establishing and sustaining a religious order. This tension was present from the very beginning, and continued to shape the development of the Franciscan movement long after Francis' death.

Francis' vision was one of total renunciation and absolute poverty. He dreamed of a brotherhood that would follow in the footsteps of Christ and the apostles, owning nothing, relying entirely on God's providence and the generosity of others. He wanted his friars to be free from all attachments, able to go anywhere and serve anyone as humble instruments of God's love.

However, translating this vision into a stable, lasting institution was a formidable challenge. As the number of friars grew, so did the practical needs of the community. There were questions of housing, food, clothing, and the basic resources needed for ministry and service.

There were also legal and canonical issues to navigate. The Church had strict rules around religious orders, their governance, and their relationship to Church authority. Fitting Francis' radical vision into these established structures was not always easy.

Francis himself struggled with these tensions. He was always hesitant to impose too many rules or structures, fearing that they would stifle the spirit of spontaneity and freedom that was central to his understanding of the Gospel life.

At the same time, he recognized the need for some level of organization and governance. He worked closely with Church authorities, especially Cardinal Hugolino (later Pope Gregory IX), to develop a rule and structure that would be acceptable to the Church while remaining true to his vision.

After Francis' death, these tensions continued to play out. Some friars, known as the "Spirituals," insisted on a strict interpretation of Francis' poverty, rejecting any form of communal property or stable residences. Others, the "Conventuals," argued for a more moderated approach, accepting the use of property and resources for the sake of the Order's life and ministry.

These debates sometimes led to bitter conflicts and even schisms within the Order. Popes and Church councils were called upon to intervene, to clarify the proper interpretation of the Franciscan rule and charism.

Over time, the Order found ways to balance Francis' ideals with the realities of institutional life. Franciscan communities developed various structures and practices to live out the spirit of poverty and simplicity while also providing for the needs of the friars and their ministries.

The Franciscan Second Order (the Poor Clares) and Third Order (lay Franciscans) also emerged, offering new ways for people to live out the Franciscan charism in different states of life.

Throughout all of these developments, Francis remained the guiding light and inspiration. His example of radical Gospel living, his love for the poor and the outcast, his joy in God's creation—these continued to be the core values that defined Franciscan identity, even as the practical expressions of those values adapted to changing times and circumstances.

Chapter 4

Teaching and Writings

The Canticle of the Sun

One of the most beloved and enduring expressions of Francis' spirituality is his "Canticle of the Sun," also known as the "Canticle of the Creatures." This poetic prayer, composed near the end of Francis' life, is a joyful, lyrical celebration of God's creation and a powerful expression of Francis' theology and worldview.

The Canticle is written in Francis' native Umbrian dialect, making it one of the earliest known works of Italian literature. Its structure is simple yet profound, with each stanza praising God for a different element of creation: the sun, the moon and stars, the wind and air, water, fire, and the earth.

What makes the Canticle remarkable is the way it expresses Francis' deep sense of kinship with all of creation. He addresses the sun, moon, and other elements as "brothers" and "sisters," reflecting his belief that all creatures are part of one family, all sharing a common divine origin and destiny.

This sense of fraternity with creation was a radical departure from the prevailing worldview of Francis' time, which often saw the material world as something to be transcended or dominated. For Francis, the natural world was not an obstacle to spirituality but a sacrament, a visible sign of God's invisible grace.

The Canticle also reflects Francis' understanding of God as the source of all goodness and beauty. Each element of creation is praised not for its own sake, but as a reflection of divine love and generosity. The sun is praised as an image of God's radiance, the water for its humility and preciousness, the earth for its nurturing sustenance.

This theological vision would later be developed by Franciscan scholars like Bonaventure and Duns Scotus, who saw the created world as a "ladder" or "book" leading the mind and heart to God. It also anticipated modern ecological spirituality, with its emphasis on the interconnectedness of all life and the sacredness of the earth.

Beyond its theological and literary significance, the Canticle also holds a special place in Franciscan tradition because of the circumstances of its composition. Francis wrote the Canticle during a time of great physical suffering, when he was nearly blind and in constant pain. Yet in the midst of this suffering, he was able to sing a song of praise, gratitude, and joy.

This spirit of joy in the face of suffering, of finding God's presence and goodness even in the midst of darkness, is a key part of Francis' spiritual legacy. The Canticle embodies this spirit perfectly, and has served as a source of inspiration and consolation for countless people over the centuries.

Today, the Canticle of the Sun continues to be widely prayed and sung in Franciscan communities and beyond. It has been set to music by numerous composers, adapted into various languages and styles, and incorporated into liturgical and devotional contexts.

More broadly, the Canticle's vision of cosmic fraternity and ecological harmony continues to resonate in our contemporary world, as we grapple with the urgent challenges of environmental degradation and climate change. Francis' words remind us of our deep connection to the earth and to each other, and call us to a renewed sense of wonder, gratitude, and responsibility for the gift of creation.

Sermons and Letters

Francis was not a scholar in the formal sense, but he was a passionate and effective communicator of the Gospel. His sermons and letters offer a vivid glimpse into his spiritual vision and his approach to ministry and leadership.

Francis' preaching was rooted in his deep immersion in Scripture. He had a particular love for the Gospels, and would often base his sermons directly on Gospel passages, inviting his listeners to enter imaginatively into the stories of Jesus' life and teachings.

His preaching style was simple, direct, and often dramatic. He would use vivid imagery, storytelling, and even physical gestures to convey his message. One famous example is his "Sermon to the Birds," in which he spontaneously began preaching to a flock of birds about God's love and care for all creatures.

This simplicity and directness of style reflected Francis' own spiritual path. He had little formal education, and distrusted the kind of scholarly learning that he felt could lead to pride and detachment from the poor. Instead, he sought to embody the Gospel in a way that was accessible and compelling to ordinary people.

At the same time, Francis' preaching was deeply challenging. He called his listeners to a radical conversion of life, to a total commitment to following Christ in poverty, humility, and love. He denounced the sins of greed, violence, and hypocrisy, and invited all people to embrace the way of penance and peace.

Francis' letters reveal a similar blend of simplicity and depth. He wrote to encourage, instruct, and sometimes admonish his brothers and followers. He also corresponded with Church leaders, including the Pope, offering his counsel and support.

One of the most significant of Francis' writings is his "Letter to All the Faithful," also known as the "Second Letter to the Faithful" or the "Volterra Letter." This letter, written near the end of Francis' life, is a kind of spiritual testament, summing up his core teachings and exhortations.

In the letter, Francis calls all Christians to a life of penance, poverty, and humility. He stresses the importance of the sacraments, especially the Eucharist, and urges his readers to love and serve one another, especially the poor and marginalized. He also warns against the dangers of sin and the urgency of preparing for death and judgment.

Throughout the letter, Francis' tone is both tender and urgent. He addresses his readers as "brothers and sisters," and expresses his deep desire for their salvation and spiritual growth. At the same time, he does not shy away from challenging them to a high standard of Gospel living.

This combination of tenderness and challenge, of simplicity and depth, is characteristic of Francis' preaching and writing as a whole. He had a rare gift for communicating profound spiritual truths in a way that touched the heart and inspired the will.

Today, Francis' sermons and letters continue to be studied and cherished by Franciscans and many others. They offer a window into the soul of a man who was wholly in love with God and with all that God has made. They challenge us to a deeper and more authentic embrace of the Gospel, and invite us to share in Francis' joy and passion for the Kingdom of God.

The Stigmata

One of the most extraordinary and controversial events in Francis' life was his reception of the stigmata, the wounds of Christ's crucifixion, in his own body. This event, which took place near the end of Francis' life, has been a source of fascination, veneration, and debate for centuries.

According to Franciscan tradition, in the year 1224, two years before his death, Francis retreated to Mount La Verna for a period of fasting and prayer. During this time, he had a vision of a seraph, a six-winged angelic being, bearing the likeness of a crucified man.

As Francis gazed upon this vision, he felt a deep sense of compassion and desire to share in Christ's sufferings. At the same time, he experienced a searing pain in his hands, feet, and side, as if he himself were being pierced by nails and a lance.

When the vision ended, Francis found that his body bore the marks of Christ's wounds. His hands and feet had what appeared to be nail holes, and his side had a wound as if pierced by a spear. These marks remained on his body for the rest of his life, and were witnessed by many of his companions and followers.

The significance of the stigmata for Francis and his followers was profound. On a spiritual level, it was seen as a sign of Francis' deep union with Christ, a physical manifestation of his interior conformity to the crucified Lord. It was a confirmation of his holiness and his role as a living icon of Christ.

On a theological level, the stigmata were interpreted in light of the Pauline concept of sharing in the sufferings of Christ. Just as Paul wrote of completing in his own body what is lacking in Christ's afflictions (Col 1:24), so Francis was seen as participating in a unique way in the redemptive passion of Christ.

The stigmata also had a powerful impact on the development of Franciscan spirituality. They reinforced the centrality of the cross and the importance of embracing suffering as a path to spiritual growth. They inspired a particular devotion to the passion of Christ and the practice of meditating on His wounds.

At the same time, the stigmata were a source of controversy and skepticism. Some questioned whether they were genuinely supernatural or whether they might have been self-inflicted or fabricated. Others worried that an excessive focus on the stigmata could distract from the core of Francis' message and example.

The Church itself was initially cautious about the stigmata. It was only after a thorough investigation that Pope Gregory IX, a friend and supporter of Francis, officially confirmed their authenticity in 1237.

Over time, however, the stigmata became an integral part of the Franciscan tradition and a key aspect of Francis' iconography.

Artistic depictions of Francis almost always include the stigmata, and the feast of the Stigmata of St. Francis is celebrated annually on September 17.

Today, the meaning and significance of the stigmata continue to be pondered by Christians of all traditions. For some, they are a powerful sign of the depths of God's love and the transformative power of union with Christ. For others, they remain a mystery, an invitation to humble contemplation of the ways of God.

Regardless of one's interpretation, the stigmata stand as a potent symbol of Francis' total identification with the poor, suffering Christ. They remind us that the path of Christian discipleship is not always easy or comfortable, but that in embracing the cross, we find the fullness of life and love.

Contributions to Christian Literature

Francis' writings, though not extensive, made a significant impact on the development of Christian literature and spirituality. His works, which include prayers, letters, rules for his communities, and the famous Canticle of the Sun, reflect his unique spiritual vision and have inspired generations of believers.

One of Francis' most important literary contributions was his role in the development of vernacular religious literature. By composing works in Italian rather than Latin, Francis made spiritual writing more accessible to ordinary people. This was part of his larger mission to democratize spirituality, to make the riches of the Gospel available to all.

The Canticle of the Sun, in particular, stands as a landmark of Italian literature. Its use of Umbrian dialect and its simple, rhythmic structure made it easy to memorize and recite. It became a model for later Italian poets and helped to establish the vernacular as a legitimate medium for spiritual expression.

Francis' writings also played a key role in shaping Franciscan spirituality and identity. His two rules for the friars minor, the "Earlier Rule" and the "Later Rule," set out the core principles and practices of Franciscan life. They emphasized radical poverty, simplicity, humility, and a life lived in imitation of Christ.

Similarly, his letters to his followers, including his Letter to All the Faithful and his letters to clergy, offered spiritual guidance and encouragement. They reveal Francis' pastoral heart and his deep desire to lead others into a deeper relationship with God.

Francis' prayers, such as the "Prayer before the Crucifix" and the "Blessing to Brother Leo," also became treasured parts of the Franciscan heritage. They are marked by a spirit of intimacy with God, a sense of wonder at God's goodness, and a desire for total self-giving.

Beyond their importance for the Franciscan tradition, Francis' writings have had a wide influence on Christian spirituality more broadly. His emphasis on poverty, simplicity, and humility challenged the excesses and worldliness of the Church in his time, and continues to serve as a prophetic witness today.

His love for creation and his sense of kinship with all creatures anticipated the development of ecological spirituality and the contemporary concern for the environment. His integration of action and contemplation, of service and prayer, offers a model for a balanced and embodied spirituality.

Numerous saints, theologians, and spiritual writers have drawn inspiration from Francis' writings. Bonaventure, Dante, Teresa of Avila, John of the Cross, and Thomas Merton are just a few examples of those who have been shaped by Franciscan spirituality.

In the 20th century, the publication of Francis' complete writings in critical editions made them more widely available for study and reflection. This has led to a renewed appreciation for Francis as a spiritual master and a guide for our times.

Today, Francis' writings continue to be read, studied, and prayed by Christians of all traditions. They offer a fresh and ever-relevant invitation to embrace the Gospel in all its radical simplicity and transformative power. They challenge us to live in right relationship with God, with each other, and with all of creation.

In a world that often values wealth, power, and self-assertion, Francis' words remind us of the beauty and joy of a life centered on love of God and neighbor. They call us back to the heart of the Christian message and inspire us to be instruments of God's peace and goodness in the world.

Chapter 5

Pilgrimages and Encounters

Journey to the Holy Land

Throughout his life, Francis had a deep love for the Holy Land, the places where Jesus had lived, preached, and died. This love was rooted in his profound desire to follow in the footsteps of Christ, to experience as closely as possible the realities of the Gospel.

In 1219, in the midst of the Fifth Crusade, Francis embarked on a pilgrimage to the Holy Land. This was a daring and dangerous undertaking, given the ongoing conflict between Christian and Muslim forces in the region.

Francis' motivation for this journey was not to participate in the Crusade, but to preach the Gospel of peace and reconciliation. He believed that the way to convert the Muslim "infidels" was not through military force, but through love, humility, and dialogue.

After a difficult sea voyage, Francis and his companion, Brother Illuminato, arrived in the port of Acre. From there, they made their way to the Crusader encampments near Damietta, in Egypt.

According to Franciscan tradition, Francis was deeply disturbed by the suffering and violence he witnessed among the Crusaders. He saw the way the war was being waged as contrary to the spirit of the Gospel, and he sought to offer a different witness.

With great courage, Francis and Illuminato crossed the battle lines and entered the camp of the Muslim Sultan, Malik al-Kamil. The exact details of this encounter are unclear, and have been embellished over time with various legends and miracles.

What seems certain is that Francis was received peacefully by the Sultan, and that the two men engaged in a respectful dialogue about faith. Francis preached the Gospel to the Sultan and his court, not seeking to condemn or convert by force, but to share the love of Christ.

The Sultan was impressed by Francis' sincerity and courage, and offered him gifts and safe passage. Francis, however, declined the gifts, remaining true to his vow of poverty.

This encounter between Francis and the Sultan became a powerful symbol of interfaith dialogue and peacemaking. It showed that even in the midst of violent conflict, it was possible to meet the "other" with respect, humility, and love.

After his time with the Sultan, Francis visited many of the holy sites associated with the life of Christ, including Bethlehem and Jerusalem. These experiences deepened his identification with the poor, humble Jesus, and his desire to conform his life totally to the Gospel.

The impact of Francis' journey to the Holy Land was significant. It marked a new phase in his spiritual journey, a deepening of his commitment to peace, poverty, and evangelization.

It also had an impact on the Franciscan Order. Francis' example inspired many of his followers to undertake similar pilgrimages and to engage in peaceful dialogue with Muslims and other non-Christians.

Today, the Franciscan Order continues to have a significant presence in the Holy Land. Franciscan friars serve as custodians of many of the holy sites, and work to promote peace, dialogue, and understanding among the peoples of the region.

Francis' pilgrimage to the Holy Land remains a powerful example of the transformative power of pilgrimage, of the way encountering the "other" can break down barriers and open up new paths of understanding and reconciliation. It invites us to embark on our own inner journeys, to follow in the footsteps of Christ with courage, humility, and love.

Encounters with Muslim Leaders

Francis' encounter with Sultan Malik al-Kamil during his pilgrimage to the Holy Land was a groundbreaking moment in Christian-Muslim relations. It demonstrated Francis' commitment to peaceful dialogue and his belief in the power of love to overcome division and conflict.

The meeting took place in 1219, during the Fifth Crusade. The Crusaders were encamped near Damietta, Egypt, preparing to attack the city. Francis and his companion, Brother Illuminato, crossed the battle lines and were taken to the Sultan's camp.

The Sultan, who was known as a wise and tolerant ruler, received Francis with respect and curiosity. He was impressed by Francis' courage in coming unarmed into the midst of his enemies, and by the sincerity of his faith.

According to Franciscan tradition, Francis preached to the Sultan and his court about the Christian faith. He did not seek to argue or condemn, but to witness to the love of Christ. He even offered to walk through fire to prove the truth of the Gospel, though the Sultan declined this offer.

The Sultan, in turn, shared with Francis about the Islamic faith. He was struck by the similarities between the two religions, particularly their common belief in one God and their emphasis on prayer and charity.

The two men engaged in a respectful and open dialogue, listening to each other and seeking to understand each other's perspectives. This was a remarkable occurrence in a time when Christians and Muslims were more often engaged in violence and demonization of the other. The encounter between Francis and the Sultan had a profound impact on both men. The Sultan was moved by Francis' genuine goodness and offered him many gifts, which Francis politely refused in keeping with his vow of poverty. Francis, for his part, was impressed by the Sultan's openness and came to see him as a fellow seeker of God.

This meeting also had a significant impact on the Franciscan Order and on Christian-Muslim relations more broadly. It showed that peaceful dialogue and mutual understanding were possible even in the midst of conflict.

Franciscan friars began to engage more actively in outreach to Muslims, learning Arabic and studying Islamic culture in order to better communicate the Gospel message. They established a presence in many Muslim-ruled lands, not as conquerors but as humble witnesses to Christ's love.

The encounter also had an influence on Islamic attitudes towards Christianity. The Sultan's respect for Francis and his willingness to engage in dialogue sent a powerful message of tolerance and openness.

In later centuries, the story of Francis and the Sultan became a popular subject for art and literature. It was seen as a model for interfaith understanding and a challenge to the crusading mentality that saw Muslims as enemies to be conquered rather than fellow human beings to be loved.

Today, in a world still riven by religious conflict and misunderstanding, the example of Francis and the Sultan remains as relevant as ever. It calls us to seek out the humanity in the other, to engage in honest and respectful dialogue, and to be willing to learn from those who are different from us.

For Francis, this encounter was a living out of the Gospel call to love one's enemies and to be a peacemaker. It was a recognition that

God's love extends to all people, and that the path to peace lies in humility, dialogue, and mutual understanding.

As we seek to build a more just and peaceful world, we can draw inspiration from Francis' courage and openness. We can strive to be instruments of dialogue and reconciliation, to see in the face of the "other" the image of God. In doing so, we too can be bearers of Christ's love in a world that so desperately needs it.

Efforts Towards Peace

Francis' encounter with Sultan Malik al-Kamil was just one example of his tireless efforts towards peace. Throughout his life, he sought to be an instrument of God's reconciling love, working to overcome division and conflict wherever he encountered it.

This commitment to peace was rooted in Francis' deep understanding of the Gospel. He saw Jesus as the Prince of Peace, the one who came to reconcile all things to God and to each other. For Francis, following Christ meant embodying this mission of reconciliation in his own life and relationships.

One of the key ways Francis worked for peace was through his emphasis on dialogue and understanding. He believed that many conflicts arose from a lack of communication and a failure to see the humanity in the other.

This is why he placed such importance on learning other languages and cultures. He encouraged his brothers to study Arabic and other languages so that they could communicate the Gospel more effectively. He also urged them to live among the people they served, to understand their ways of life and to build relationships of trust and respect.

Francis also worked for peace through his witness of radical poverty and humility. He believed that many conflicts were rooted in greed, pride, and the desire for power. By renouncing these things in his own life, he sought to show a different way of being in the world. This witness was powerful and attractive. Many people, from all walks of life, were drawn to Francis' example of simplicity and love. They saw in him a living embodiment of the Gospel, a sign of hope in a world torn by violence and division.

Francis' peacemaking efforts extended beyond the religious sphere. He also sought to bring reconciliation in social and political conflicts. One famous example is his intervention in the conflict between the mayor and bishop of Assisi.

When the mayor began to construct a wall that encroached on the bishop's land, a bitter dispute arose. Francis, who was respected by both sides, acted as a mediator. He invited both parties to meet with him at the site of the disputed wall.

There, Francis began to sing his "Canticle of the Sun," with its praise for all of God's creation. The beauty of the song and the spirit of unity it evoked had a profound effect on those present. The mayor and bishop were moved to reconcile and the wall was taken down. This story illustrates Francis' belief in the power of beauty, creativity, and prayer to overcome division. For him, peacemaking was not just a matter of negotiation or compromise, but of tapping into a deeper spirit of unity and love.

Francis' legacy as a peacemaker continues to inspire the Franciscan Order and the wider Church today. Franciscan friars are active in many areas of conflict around the world, working for reconciliation and understanding.

The Franciscan tradition of dialogue, respect for other cultures, and interfaith cooperation is more relevant than ever in our globalized, pluralistic world. It offers a model for how to build bridges of understanding and to work for the common good.

At the same time, Francis' witness of radical poverty and humility challenges us to examine the root causes of conflict in our world. It calls us to work for justice, to stand in solidarity with the poor and marginalized, and to renounce the greed and pride that so often lead to violence.

As we seek to be peacemakers in our own time, we can draw strength and inspiration from Francis' example. We can strive to be instruments of God's reconciling love, to see the face of Christ in all people, and to work tirelessly for a world where all can live in dignity, justice, and peace.

Lessons from Interfaith Dialogues

Francis' encounters with Muslim leaders, particularly his meeting with Sultan Malik al-Kamil, offer rich lessons for interfaith dialogue today. In a world where religious differences often lead to misunderstanding, mistrust, and even violence, Francis' example provides a model of respectful, open-hearted engagement with the religious other.

One of the key lessons from Francis' approach is the importance of humility and respect. Francis did not enter into dialogue with the Sultan with the intention of arguing or proving the superiority of the Christian faith. Rather, he approached the encounter with a spirit of openness and a willingness to listen and learn.

This humility allowed Francis to see the Sultan as a fellow human being, a seeker of God, rather than simply as a representative of a rival religion. It enabled him to build a relationship of mutual respect and understanding, even in the midst of a hostile and polarized environment.

Another important lesson is the centrality of witness. Francis did not engage in theological debates or intellectual arguments. Rather, he sought to communicate the Gospel through the witness of his own life and actions.

This witness was marked by radical simplicity, poverty, and love. Francis' willingness to cross battle lines unarmed, his refusal of the Sultan's gifts, his treatment of all people with equal respect and compassion - these actions spoke louder than any words.

This suggests that interfaith dialogue is not just about exchanging ideas or reaching theological agreements. It is about embodying one's faith in a way that communicates its deepest values and invites others into a shared space of encounter and understanding.

A third lesson is the importance of finding common ground. Despite the significant differences between Christianity and Islam, Francis and the Sultan were able to connect through their shared belief in one God, their commitment to prayer and charity, and their desire for peace.

This highlights the importance of focusing on what unites rather than what divides in interfaith encounters. While not ignoring or downplaying real differences, it is essential to identify the shared values and aspirations that can serve as a basis for mutual understanding and cooperation.

A fourth lesson is the transformative power of encounter. Francis' meeting with the Sultan changed both men. It broadened their understanding, challenged their stereotypes, and opened up new possibilities for relationship.

This suggests that interfaith dialogue has the potential to be deeply transformative, not just for the individuals involved but for the wider communities they represent. By building relationships of understanding and trust, dialogue can help to break down barriers, dispel misunderstandings, and create new spaces for collaboration and peacebuilding.

Finally, Francis' approach highlights the importance of courage and risk-taking. Crossing battle lines to meet with the Sultan was a dangerous and countercultural act. It required great faith, trust in God, and a willingness to step out of one's comfort zone.

This suggests that authentic interfaith dialogue requires a certain boldness, a willingness to take risks for the sake of building peace and understanding. It means being willing to challenge the prejudices and fears of one's own community, to reach out across boundaries, and to trust in the power of God's love to overcome division.

These lessons from Francis' interfaith encounters remain deeply relevant today. In a world where religious tensions and conflicts often dominate the headlines, Francis' example offers a different way forward - a path of humility, respect, witness, common ground, transformation, and courage.

As we seek to build a more just and peaceful world, we are called to follow in Francis' footsteps, to be instruments of dialogue and reconciliation, and to trust in the power of encounter to transform hearts and communities. In doing so, we can help to build bridges of understanding and to create a world where diversity is celebrated and where all people can live together in harmony and peace.

Encounters with Other Faith Traditions

While Francis' most famous interfaith encounter was with the Muslim Sultan, his spirit of openness and respect extended to other faith traditions as well. Though living in a time when religious differences were often a source of conflict and mistrust, Francis sought to build bridges of understanding wherever he could.

One example of this can be seen in Francis' encounter with a Jewish man during his pilgrimage to the Holy Land. According to Franciscan tradition, Francis was walking through a Jewish quarter in a city along his way when he came upon a man who was very ill.

Moved with compassion, Francis stopped to care for the man, washing his wounds and offering him comfort. The man was deeply touched by Francis' kindness, and a bond of friendship formed between them.

Francis' openness to other faith traditions was also evident in his approach to evangelization. Unlike many of his contemporaries, who sought to convert non-Christians through force or coercion, Francis emphasized the importance of witness and example. He instructed his brothers to live among the people they served, to learn their languages and customs, and to share the Gospel through the quality of their lives. He believed that the most effective way to draw others to Christ was through love, humility, and service.

This approach had a significant impact on the Franciscan missions of the 13th and 14th centuries. Franciscan friars were among the first Europeans to venture into the Mongol Empire and to establish a presence in China. They sought to engage in respectful dialogue with the people they met, learning from their wisdom and sharing the beauty of the Christian faith.

Francis' spirit of interfaith openness also shaped his understanding of the created world. He saw all of nature as a reflection of God's goodness and beauty, and he believed that God's presence could be discerned in all things.

This led him to a deep respect for the religious traditions of indigenous peoples, who often had a strong sense of the sacredness of nature. Rather than seeking to eradicate these traditions, Francis and his followers sought to find points of connection and to incorporate elements of indigenous spirituality into their own understanding of the Gospel.

This spirit of inculturation, of respectfully engaging with and learning from the wisdom of other cultures, became a hallmark of the Franciscan tradition. It reflects Francis' belief in the universality of God's love and in the need for the Church to be in dialogue with the world.

Today, this aspect of Francis' legacy continues to inspire Franciscans and other Christians in their interfaith efforts. It challenges us to approach religious differences with humility, respect, and a willingness to learn.

Chapter 6

Final Years and Death

Declining Health

In the last years of his life, Francis of Assisi's health declined sharply due to a combination of factors. The rigorous austerities he had practiced throughout his life, his frequent fasting, his long journeys on foot, and the cold and damp conditions in which he often lived all took their toll on his body. Moreover, the stigmata that Francis had received two years before his death caused him great physical pain. The wounds in his hands, feet, and side would often bleed and become infected, adding to his sufferings.

Francis also suffered from a severe eye infection, likely trachoma, which caused him intense pain and gradually robbed him of his sight. In his later years, he was nearly blind, able only to perceive light and shadows. Despite these physical afflictions, Francis sought to embrace his sufferings as a participation in the passion of Christ.

He saw his bodily weakness as an opportunity to rely more fully on God's grace and to identify more closely with the poor and marginalized.

Francis' attitude towards his own suffering was consistent with his overall spirituality. He believed that the path to spiritual growth and union with God often led through the valley of suffering and self-denial. By embracing the cross in his own life, Francis sought to conform himself more fully to Christ. At the same time, Francis did not glorify suffering for its own sake. He sought medical care when it was available and accepted the help and comfort offered by his brothers. He also continued to find joy and consolation in prayer, in the beauty of creation, and in the fellowship of his community.

The Last Days

One of the most remarkable testaments to Francis' spirit in the face of suffering is his "Canticle of the Sun," composed during a time of great physical pain. In this hymn, Francis praises God for the beauty and goodness of all creation, seeing in each element a reflection of the divine love. The Canticle is a powerful expression of Francis' unshakeable faith and his ability to find God's presence even in the midst of darkness and pain. It reflects his deep conviction that all of life, including suffering, has meaning and purpose in God's redemptive plan.

As Francis' health continued to decline, he retired to a small hut near the church of San Damiano, where he could pray and reflect in solitude. This location held special significance for Francis, as it was near the place where he had first heard Christ's call to rebuild the Church. Even in his weakened state, however, Francis continued to offer guidance and inspiration to his followers. He urged them to remain faithful to their calling, to embrace poverty and humility, and to always put the love of God and neighbor above all else.

Francis' last days were marked by a deep longing for union with Christ. He saw his sufferings as a participation in the Lord's passion and welcomed them as a gift. "Welcome, Sister Death," he is reported to have said, seeing in his own passing a doorway to eternal life.

Death of Francis

On the evening of October 3, 1226, at the age of 44, Francis of Assisi passed from this life to the next. As he lay on his deathbed, he asked to be placed naked on the ground, in ultimate solidarity with the poor and with the earth he had so loved. Surrounded by his brothers, he listened as the Passion narrative from the Gospel of John was read aloud. When the reading came to the verse, "They took the body of Jesus and bound it in linen cloths with the spices, as is the burial custom of the Jews" (John 19:40), Francis lifted his hand in blessing, thanking God for the gift of Sister Death. As he breathed his last, Francis recited Psalm 141, "I cry to you, O Lord; I say, 'You are my refuge, my portion in the land of the living.'" With the final words of the psalm, "Bring my soul out of prison, so that I may give thanks to your name," Francis passed into eternal life.

The immediate reaction to Francis' death was one of both grief and awe. The brothers who had been with him were overcome with sorrow at the loss of their beloved father and guide. At the same time, they couldn't help but be struck by the holiness and peace that seemed to emanate from Francis even in death. Word of Francis' passing spread quickly throughout Assisi and beyond. Crowds of people, from the poorest beggars to the wealthiest nobles, flocked to the Porziuncola chapel to pay their respects to the man they had come to revere as a saint. Many miracles were reported in the days and weeks following Francis' death. People who touched his body or his tomb were said to have been healed of various illnesses and infirmities. These miracles were seen as a confirmation of Francis' sanctity and a sign of God's continued presence and power.

Immediate Impact

The impact of Francis' death was immediate and profound. Just two years after his death, Pope Gregory IX canonized him, declaring him a model of Christian virtue and a patron of the Church. Yet even as the Church celebrated Francis' sanctity, his followers grappled with the challenge of remaining faithful to his vision. In the years following his death, debates and divisions would emerge within the Franciscan Order, as different factions sought to interpret and apply

Francis' legacy in different ways. Some brothers, known as the "Spirituals," argued for a strict, literal observance of Francis' rule of poverty. They saw any compromise or accommodation as a betrayal of Francis' vision. Other brothers, known as the "Conventuals," advocated for a more moderate approach, allowing for the use of property and resources for the sake of the Order's life and ministry. These tensions would continue to play out in the years and decades following Francis' death, sometimes leading to bitter conflicts and even schisms within the Order.

Despite these challenges, the core of Francis' message and example continued to inspire and guide the Franciscan movement. His radical embrace of poverty, his joy in the Gospel, his love for all creatures, his commitment to peace - these remained the hallmarks of Franciscan spirituality. Francis' death also had a profound impact on the wider Church and society. His life and example had offered a powerful challenge to the values of his time, a call to return to the simplicity and poverty of the Gospel. His witness would continue to inspire reform movements and renewal efforts throughout the history of the Church.

In his death, as in his life, Francis pointed beyond himself to the God he had so faithfully served. He had sought to be a living icon of Christ, to embody in his own flesh the mystery of the cross and resurrection. As he passed from this world to the next, he invited all people to share in that same mystery, to find in Christ the source of all life and hope. Today, as we remember Francis' holy death, we are called to take up his mantle, to continue his work of living the Gospel in simplicity, joy, and love. May we, like Francis, be instruments of God's peace and mercy in a world that so desperately needs to know the love of Christ.

Chapter 7

Legacy and Lessons

Impact on the Church

The life and legacy of Saint Francis of Assisi had a profound and lasting impact on the Catholic Church. His radical commitment to poverty, simplicity, and humility challenged the Church of his day and continues to inspire reform and renewal efforts to this day.

One of the most significant ways in which Francis impacted the Church was through the establishment of the Franciscan Order. This religious community, founded on Francis' vision and rule of life, quickly grew and spread throughout Europe and beyond.

The Franciscans became one of the most influential religious orders in the history of the Church. They were known for their commitment to poverty, their service to the poor and marginalized, and their dedication to preaching the Gospel in a simple and accessible way.

Through the Franciscan Order, Francis' spirit and values were embedded into the institutional life of the Church. Franciscan friars and sisters served in a variety of roles - as preachers, confessors, theologians, missionaries, and more. They helped to shape the spiritual and intellectual life of the Church in significant ways.

Beyond the Franciscan Order itself, Francis' example inspired a broader movement of spiritual renewal within the Church. His life and teachings emphasized a return to the simplicity and poverty of the Gospel, a focus on the humanity of Christ, and a love for all of God's creation.

These themes resonated deeply with many Christians who were seeking a more authentic and vibrant faith. Francis' example inspired numerous other religious orders and lay movements that sought to live out the Gospel in a more radical and committed way.

The Franciscan emphasis on poverty and simplicity also had a significant impact on the Church's understanding of its mission and role in the world. Francis challenged the Church to embrace a spirit of humility and service, to be a Church of and for the poor.

This challenge was taken up in various ways throughout the history of the Church. It can be seen in the development of Catholic social teaching, in the emergence of liberation theology, and in the renewed emphasis on the Church's preferential option for the poor in the 20th and 21st centuries.

Francis' impact on the Church was not without its tensions and challenges. His radical vision of poverty and simplicity was not always easily reconciled with the institutional needs and realities of the Church. The divisions within the Franciscan Order itself, between the Spirituals and the Conventuals, reflected these ongoing tensions.

Nevertheless, Francis' legacy continues to be a vital source of inspiration and renewal for the Church. In his simplicity and humility, he points the Church back to the heart of the Gospel message. In his love for the poor and marginalized, he reminds the Church of its fundamental mission. In his joy and wonder at the beauty of creation, he invites the Church to embrace a more integral and holistic spirituality.

In recent years, Pope Francis, who took his papal name in honor of Saint Francis of Assisi, has sought to renew the Church in the spirit of his namesake. His emphasis on simplicity, poverty, mercy, and care for creation echoes the core themes of Franciscan spirituality.

As the Church continues to face new challenges and opportunities in the 21st century, the example and wisdom of Saint Francis remain as relevant as ever. His life and legacy invite us to a continual conversion of heart, a deeper embrace of the Gospel, and a more authentic witness to the love and mercy of God.

May the Church continue to draw from the rich well of Franciscan spirituality, finding in Francis' example a perennial source of renewal, hope, and joy. May we, like Francis, become ever more conformed to Christ, living signs of God's love in a world that so desperately needs to experience that love.

Ongoing Influence

The influence of the Franciscan movement, initiated by Saint Francis of Assisi in the early 13th century, has continued to shape the Church and the world in significant ways over the past 800 years. The Franciscan charism, with its emphasis on poverty, simplicity, service, and love for all creation, has proven to be a perennial source of inspiration and renewal.

One of the most visible ways in which the Franciscan movement continues to influence the Church is through the various Franciscan orders and communities that exist today. The First Order, which includes the Order of Friars Minor (OFM), the Capuchins (OFM Cap.), and the Conventuals (OFM Conv.), continues to be a significant presence in the life of the Church.

Franciscan friars serve in a wide variety of ministries - as parish priests, chaplains, teachers, scholars, missionaries, and more. They are known for their commitment to simplicity of life, their solidarity with the poor and marginalized, and their efforts to promote peace, justice, and care for creation.

The Second Order, the Poor Clares, and the Third Order, which includes both religious and lay members, also continue to embody the Franciscan charism in their own unique ways. The Poor Clares, the contemplative women's branch of the Franciscan family, live a life of prayer, poverty, and enclosure, interceding for the needs of the Church and the world. The Third Order, also known as the Secular Franciscan Order, allows lay people to live out the Franciscan spirit in their daily lives and secular professions.

Beyond these formal Franciscan orders, the influence of Franciscan spirituality can be seen in numerous other movements and initiatives within the Church. Many new religious communities and lay associations have drawn inspiration from Francis' example, adapting the Franciscan charism to the particular needs and contexts of their time and place.

The Franciscan intellectual tradition has also continued to shape Catholic theology and spirituality. Great Franciscan thinkers like Saint Bonaventure and Blessed John Duns Scotus developed unique theological and philosophical perspectives that emphasized the primacy of love, the goodness of creation, and the centrality of Christ.

In recent years, there has been a renewed interest in the Franciscan intellectual tradition, particularly in light of contemporary ecological and social challenges. Franciscan thought offers a rich resource for developing a more integral and relational understanding of the human person, the created world, and our place within the cosmic community of creation.

The Franciscan commitment to dialogue, peace, and interfaith understanding has also taken on new relevance in our increasingly globalized and pluralistic world. The famous encounter between Francis and the Sultan during the Crusades has become an iconic symbol of the possibility of peaceful encounter and mutual respect between religions.

Today, Franciscans are actively involved in interfaith dialogue and peacemaking efforts around the world. They seek to promote a culture of encounter, where differences are respected and the common humanity of all people is affirmed.

Perhaps one of the most significant ways in which the Franciscan movement continues to influence the Church and the world is through the powerful witness of Franciscan saints and blessed throughout the centuries. From Saint Clare of Assisi to Saint Padre Pio, from Saint Maximilian Kolbe to Saint Marianne Cope, Franciscan men and women have embodied the Gospel in radical and transformative ways.

These Franciscan saints and blessed, coming from diverse contexts and living out the Franciscan charism in unique ways, serve as perennial sources of inspiration and challenge. They remind us of the call to holiness that is at the heart of the Christian life, and they invite us to a continual conversion of heart and life.

As the Church and the world face the challenges of the 21st century, the Franciscan movement remains a vital source of wisdom, hope, and renewal. In a world marked by violence, division, inequality, and ecological destruction, the Franciscan emphasis on simplicity, poverty, peace, and love for all creation is more relevant than ever.

May the ongoing influence of the Franciscan movement continue to shape the Church and the world in the direction of the Gospel. May we all be inspired by the example of Saint Francis and the Franciscan saints to live more authentically, love more deeply, and work more tirelessly for the coming of God's kingdom of justice, peace, and joy.

Cultural and Environmental Contributions

The influence of Saint Francis of Assisi and the Franciscan movement extends far beyond the realm of the Church. Francis' life and vision have had a profound impact on Western culture, art, literature, and, more recently, on environmental thought and activism.

In the realm of art, Francis' life and the early Franciscan movement provided a wealth of new subjects and themes. The poverty and simplicity of Francis' life, his love for nature, his receiving of the stigmata, and the vibrant narratives of the early Franciscan communities inspired artists for centuries.

The great Italian painter Giotto di Bondone, in his famous frescoes in the Basilica of Saint Francis in Assisi, helped to establish a new artistic paradigm. His naturalistic and emotionally expressive depictions of Francis' life set the stage for the development of Renaissance art.

Countless other artists, from Cimabue to Caravaggio, from El Greco to Zurbarán, found in Francis a compelling subject. Through their works, they helped to spread the Franciscan spirit and values throughout European culture.

In the field of literature, Francis' life and the early Franciscan movement also left a significant mark. Francis' own writings, particularly his Canticle of the Sun, are considered masterpieces of early Italian literature. They introduced a new vernacular spirituality that emphasized simplicity, joy, and praise.

The early Franciscan movement also produced significant literary works, such as The Little Flowers of Saint Francis and The Sacred Exchange between Saint Francis and Lady Poverty. These works, which blend history, legend, and spiritual allegory, helped to shape the popular image of Francis and the Franciscan ideal.

Francis' influence can also be seen in the works of many great writers and poets, from Dante to Chesterton. His life and spirit have served as a perennial source of literary inspiration, embodying themes of love, simplicity, humility, and the search for authentic existence.

Perhaps one of the most significant cultural contributions of Francis and the Franciscan tradition in recent times has been in the area of environmental thought and ethics. Francis' deep love and respect for all creatures, his sense of kinship with the natural world, and his vision of a cosmic fraternity have taken on new relevance in light of the ecological crises of our time.

Francis' Canticle of the Sun, with its praise of Brother Sun, Sister Moon, Brother Wind, Sister Water, and Mother Earth, expresses a profound ecological sensitivity. It invites us to see the natural world not as a mere resource to be exploited, but as a family to be loved and cherished.

This Franciscan vision of creation has inspired numerous environmental thinkers and activists. The American cultural historian Lynn White, in his influential essay "The Historical Roots of Our Ecological Crisis," pointed to Francis as a model for a new ecological consciousness.

Pope John Paul II named Francis the patron saint of ecology in 1979, recognizing his significant contribution to environmental thought and ethics. More recently, Pope Francis, in his encyclical Laudato Si', drew heavily on the Franciscan tradition in articulating an integral ecology that links care for the poor with care for the Earth.

Today, Franciscan communities and ministries around the world are at the forefront of environmental activism and education. They seek to promote a Franciscan vision of ecology that emphasizes simplicity, sustainability, reverence for creation, and solidarity with the poor and marginalized.

As the world faces the urgent challenges of climate change, biodiversity loss, and environmental degradation, the Franciscan tradition offers a rich resource for developing a more integral and sustainable approach to living on the Earth.

May the cultural and environmental legacy of Saint Francis continue to inspire and challenge us. May we learn from his example of love and respect for all creatures, his spirit of simplicity and joy, and his vision of a world where all beings are brothers and sisters, united in the great cosmic community of creation.

Patron of Animals and Ecology

One of the most beloved and well-known aspects of Saint Francis of Assisi's legacy is his role as the patron saint of animals and ecology. This association is rooted in Francis' deep love and respect for all creatures, which he saw as brothers and sisters, reflecting the beauty and goodness of God.

Many stories and legends from Francis' life highlight his special connection with animals. Perhaps the most famous is the story of Francis preaching to the birds. According to this account, Francis came upon a large flock of birds and began to preach to them about God's love and care. The birds, it is said, listened attentively and did not fly away until Francis blessed them.

Another well-known story tells of Francis taming the wolf of Gubbio. This fierce wolf had been terrorizing the town, but Francis, through his gentleness and compassion, was able to make peace between the wolf and the townspeople.

These stories, whether historically accurate or not, convey a fundamental truth about Francis' approach to the natural world. He saw animals not as inferior beings or mere resources, but as creatures endowed with their own dignity and value, capable of reflecting and praising God in their own unique ways.

This attitude of respect and kinship with all creatures was rooted in Francis' deep understanding of the Gospel. He saw Christ present in all things, and he understood the Incarnation as God's affirmation of the goodness and value of the material world.

For Francis, serving and caring for the vulnerable - whether human or animal - was a way of serving and honoring Christ. He extended the Christian ethic of love and compassion to all creatures, recognizing them as part of God's beloved creation.

This aspect of Francis' spirituality has taken on new significance in light of the ecological crises of our time. In a world where species are going extinct at an alarming rate, where animal habitats are being destroyed, and where animals are often treated as mere commodities, Francis' example of reverence and care for all creatures is more relevant than ever.

The Franciscan tradition has long emphasized the importance of responsible stewardship of creation. This includes a commitment to the protection and care of animals, recognizing their intrinsic value and their place in the web of creation.

Today, many Franciscan communities and ministries are actively involved in animal welfare and conservation efforts. They work to promote a culture of respect for all life, advocating for more humane and sustainable practices in areas like agriculture, research, and wildlife management.

Francis' role as the patron saint of ecology is closely linked to his love for animals. His vision of a cosmic fraternity, where all creatures are brothers and sisters, provides a powerful foundation for a more integral and holistic approach to environmental ethics.

In his Canticle of the Sun, Francis praises God through all creatures - sun and moon, wind and water, fire and earth. He recognizes the interdependence and sacredness of all creation, and he calls us to a spirit of humility, gratitude, and care in our relationship with the natural world.

This Franciscan ecological vision has inspired countless individuals and movements committed to environmental justice and sustainability. It challenges us to rethink our place in the universe, not as dominators or exploiters, but as humble servants and co-creators, called to cherish and protect the gift of creation.

As we face the urgent challenges of climate change, biodiversity loss, pollution, and environmental degradation, the example and wisdom of Saint Francis offer a path forward. They invite us to a ecological conversion, a transformation of heart and mind that leads to new ways of living and relating to the Earth and all its creatures.

May we learn from Francis' example of love and respect for animals, his sense of kinship with all creatures, and his vision of a world where all beings are cherished and protected. May we be inspired to work for a more just, sustainable, and compassionate world, where the cry of the Earth and the cry of the poor are heard and heeded.

Art, Literature, and Environmental movements

The life and spirit of Saint Francis of Assisi have had a profound and enduring impact on art, literature, and environmental movements. Francis' radical witness to the Gospel, his love for all creatures, and his vision of a cosmic fraternity have inspired creative expressions and activist initiatives that have shaped Western culture in significant ways.

In the realm of art, Francis and the early Franciscan movement provided a rich source of inspiration for countless artists. The poverty and simplicity of Francis' life, his receiving of the stigmata, his love for nature, and the vibrant narratives of the early Franciscan communities offered new subjects and themes for artistic exploration.

The frescoes of Giotto di Bondone in the Basilica of Saint Francis in Assisi are perhaps the most famous artistic depictions of Francis' life. Giotto's naturalistic and emotionally expressive style helped to usher in a new era of artistic realism and humanism.

Throughout the centuries, artists as diverse as Cimabue, Bellini, Caravaggio, El Greco, Rubens, and Zurbarán found in Francis a compelling subject. Through their paintings, sculptures, and other works, they helped to spread the Franciscan spirit and values throughout European culture.

Francis' influence is also evident in the development of the Italian Renaissance. His emphasis on the goodness of the material world, his affirmation of individual experience, and his use of the vernacular language in his writings and prayers all contributed to the humanistic spirit of the Renaissance.

In the field of literature, Francis and the Franciscan tradition have left an equally significant mark. Francis' own writings, particularly his Canticle of the Sun, are considered masterpieces of early Italian literature. They introduce a new vernacular spirituality that emphasizes simplicity, joy, and praise.

The early Franciscan movement also produced significant literary works, such as The Little Flowers of Saint Francis and The Sacred

Exchange between Saint Francis and Lady Poverty. These works blend history, legend, and spiritual allegory, and they helped to shape the popular image of Francis and the Franciscan ideal.

Francis' life and spirit have served as a source of inspiration for numerous writers and poets throughout the centuries. Dante, in his Divine Comedy, places Francis in the highest sphere of Paradise, praising him as a "sun" that illuminated the world. Other writers, from Chaucer to Kazantzakis, from Chesterton to Zeffirelli, have found in Francis a model of authentic Christian living and a source of literary inspiration.

Conclusion

The life and teachings of St. Francis of Assisi continue to resonate deeply within the Catholic Church and beyond, offering timeless lessons in humility, simplicity, and profound spirituality. Francis' radical commitment to poverty, his deep love for creation, and his unwavering dedication to living out the Gospel have left an indelible mark on the Church. The establishment of the Franciscan Order, which rapidly grew and spread across Europe, stands as a testament to his enduring influence. Through the Franciscan friars and sisters who serve in various capacities—preachers, theologians, missionaries, and more—Francis' spirit of poverty and service has been woven into the fabric of the Church's mission. His emphasis on simplicity and humility continues to challenge the Church to return to the core values of the Gospel, fostering a spirit of renewal and reform.

Beyond the institutional impact, St. Francis' example of love for all creatures and his vision of a cosmic fraternity have inspired countless movements and initiatives aimed at fostering peace, justice, and environmental stewardship. His "Canticle of the Sun" and other writings reflect a profound ecological consciousness, urging a respectful and harmonious relationship with the natural world. Today, as the Church navigates the complexities of the modern world, Francis' teachings remain a vital source of inspiration, reminding us of the importance of humility, compassion, and a deep reverence for all of God's creation. As we strive to address contemporary challenges, the wisdom and legacy of St. Francis of Assisi continue to guide us towards a more just, sustainable, and spiritually enriched future. May his example inspire us to live out the Gospel with renewed fervor, embracing simplicity, service, and a deep love for all creation.

Appendices

A. Glossary of Technical Terms and Concepts

A. Glossary of Medieval Terms and Concepts

Canticle of the Sun: Also known as the "Canticle of the Creatures," this is a religious song composed by Saint Francis of Assisi. It expresses his belief in the interconnectedness of all creation and praises God through various elements of nature.

Conventuals: A branch of the Franciscan Order that emerged in the 13th century. They were more open to a moderate interpretation of Francis' rule, especially regarding the vow of poverty.

Franciscan Order: The religious order founded by Saint Francis of Assisi in the early 13th century. It is characterized by its commitment to poverty, simplicity, and service to others.

Friary: A monastery or religious house of friars, particularly in the Franciscan Order.

Incarnation: The Christian belief that God became flesh in the person of Jesus Christ. For Francis, this affirmed the goodness and value of the material world.

Laity: Members of the Church who are not ordained as clergy. The Franciscan Third Order includes lay members who commit to living out Franciscan values in their daily lives.

Mendicant: A term used to describe religious orders, like the Franciscans, who rely on charitable donations and begging for their livelihood.

Poor Clares: The Second Order of the Franciscan family, founded by Saint Clare of Assisi. They are a contemplative order of women who live a life of prayer, poverty, and enclosure.

Rule: A set of guidelines or principles that govern the life of a religious order. The Franciscan Rule, based on the teachings of Saint Francis, emphasizes poverty, chastity, and obedience.

Secular Franciscan Order: Formerly known as the Third Order of Saint Francis, this is an order for lay people who seek to live out Franciscan spirituality in their daily lives.

Spirituals: A movement within the Franciscan Order that advocated for a strict interpretation of Francis' rule, especially regarding the vow of poverty.

Stigmata: The wounds corresponding to those of the crucified Christ. Saint Francis is said to have miraculously received the stigmata in 1224.

B. Timeline

1181/1182 - Francis is born in Assisi, Italy, to a wealthy cloth merchant family.

1202 - Francis takes part in a war between Assisi and Perugia and is taken prisoner. He spends a year in captivity.

1204 - After a period of illness and spiritual crisis, Francis has a vision of Christ and begins to change his way of life.

1205 - Francis renounces his father's wealth in a public square in Assisi.

1208 - While attending Mass, Francis hears the Gospel call to a life of itinerant preaching and decides to dedicate himself wholly to a life of poverty.

1209 - Francis and his early followers travel to Rome, where Pope Innocent III gives verbal approval for their way of life.

1212 - Clare of Assisi joins Francis' movement, leading to the foundation of the Poor Clares, the Second Franciscan Order.

1219 - During the Fifth Crusade, Francis travels to Egypt and meets with Sultan Malik al-Kamil, seeking to end the conflict and spread the Gospel message.

1223 - Pope Honorius III gives formal approval to the Franciscan Rule.

1224 - While in prayer on Mount La Verna, Francis receives the stigmata, the wounds of Christ.

1226 - On October 3, Francis dies in the Porziuncola, the chapel where his movement began.

1228 - Francis is canonized by Pope Gregory IX.

C. Further Reading and Resources

Books

"The Complete Works of Francis of Assisi" - A collection of Francis' writings, including his rules, letters, prayers, and the Canticle of the Sun.

"Francis of Assisi: A New Biography" by Augustine Thompson - A scholarly and comprehensive biography that seeks to separate historical fact from legend.

"The Road to Assisi: The Essential Biography of St. Francis" by Paul Sabatier - A classic biography that played a significant role in reviving interest in Francis in the early 20th century.

"The Franciscan Tradition" by William Short - An overview of Franciscan spirituality, its history, key figures, and core values.

"Care for Creation: A Franciscan Spirituality of the Earth" by Ilia Delio, Keith Douglass Warner, and Pamela Wood - An exploration of Franciscan ecological thought and its relevance for today's environmental crises.

"Franciscan Prayer" by Ilia Delio - An introduction to the richness of the Franciscan prayer tradition.

"The Franciscans: A History" by Michael Robson - A comprehensive history of the Franciscan Order from its origins to the present day.

Websites

FranciscanMedia.org - A website offering resources on Franciscan spirituality, including articles, videos, and podcasts.

FranciscanAction.org - The website of Franciscan Action Network, an organization dedicated to Franciscan-inspired social justice and advocacy.

FranciscanEarth.org - A resource for exploring the Franciscan perspective on ecology and care for creation.

Thank you for reading this book. Please write a review, and share with your friends on social media if you enjoyed this title.
We are counting on you to spread the word!

If you liked this book, you will also enjoy new and upcoming titles from our Great Explorers series about extraordinary adventurers like Ferdinand Magellan, Ernest Shackleton, Roald Amundsen, Marco Polo, and others!

Explore more titles from Lexicon Labs in the pages that follow.

Don't forget to sign up to our newsletter and download your FREE poster print! Go to https://mindzen.squarespace.com/ and sign up today!

Explore the lives of great innovators, Scientists, Leaders, Artists and Explorers...Stay tuned for additional titles coming soon!

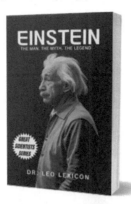

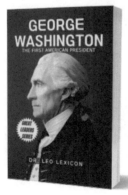

Learn the basics of Coding and program in Python.
No prior knowledge required!

Meet our bestselling titles on AI
BOOKS FOR CURIOUS MINDS

- Structured introduction to the building blocks of AI
- Review of major milestones in AI history
- Meet the leading inventors and their key innovations
- AI concepts explained in a simple, easy-to-understand format by a Bay Area educator
- Resources for puzzles, games, and coding
- Perfect travel companion or gift

Follow Dr. Leo Lexicon on Twitter/X

 @LeoLexicon

LEXICON LABS

LEARN ALL ABOUT STARTING AND GROWING A BUSINESS AS A TEENAGER

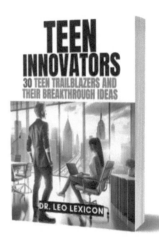

Explore the Future of Quantum Computing

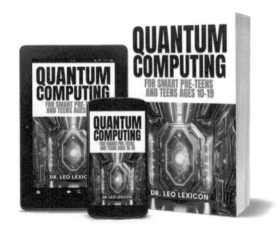

FUN BOOKS FOR TRIVIA NIGHT

COLORING BOOKS

TEST YOUR INNER NERD!

Made in United States
Troutdale, OR
11/20/2024

25102232R00060